U.S. Secret Service Secrets

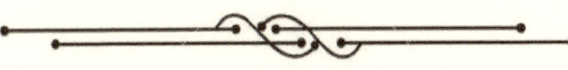

Interesting Facts About

American Agents and Their

Service to the Nation

Michelle L. Fischer

Bluesource And Friends

This book is brought to you by Bluesource And Friends, a happy book publishing company.

Our motto is **"Happiness Within Pages"**
We promise to deliver amazing value to readers with our books.
We also appreciate honest book reviews from our readers.

Connect with us on our Facebook page www.facebook.com/bluesourceandfriends and stay tuned to our latest book promotions and free giveaways.

Don't forget to claim your FREE books!

Brain Teasers:

https://tinyurl.com/karenbrainteasers

Harry Potter Trivia:

https://tinyurl.com/wizardworldtrivia

Sherlock Puzzle Book (Volume 2)

https://tinyurl.com/Sherlockpuzzlebook2

Also check out our best seller book

"67 Lateral Thinking Puzzles"

https://tinyurl.com/thinkingandriddles

Contents

U.S. Secret Service Secrets

Introduction

Thank you for getting *U.S. Secret Service Secrets: Interesting Facts About American Agents and Their Service to the Nation*. It's a book that is chock full of information and some surprises about the U.S. Secret Service.

The book will cover the history of the U.S. Secret Service, from its formation by the authorization signed by Abraham Lincoln earlier in the day prior to his assassination the evening of April 14, 1865, to its present-day service protecting the president, vice president, their families, and visiting dignitaries from around the world. The Secret Service is still involved in rooting out money counterfeiters, cyber fraud, and many other frauds and dangers that are active and part of the world we live in today.

The Secret Service has been a revered institution and has served the nation in good stead as protectors, as well as their involvement in many other facets of the

government. This book has been written not only as an informative piece about the agency, but one that will give the reader insight into some of the fun facts and experiences that are part of the history of the Secret Service, and the men and women who have worked in this organization.

It has been a pleasure writing about the elite U.S. Secret Service and the American agents who serve the President and Vice President of the country. Every effort was made to ensure to bring you a book that's as informative as possible. Please enjoy!

Chapter 1: The U.S. Secret Service — Its History and the Qualities and Qualifications to Be Accepted into the Service

The United State Secret Service. Just saying this phrase brings to mind the elite group men and women who bring a special service that is afforded to the President of the United States, the Vice President, and their immediate families. They are also responsible to protect former Presidents and their spouses and any family members under 16 years of age. In addition, they are assigned to major presidential and vice presidential candidates and their spouses, visiting dignitaries from other countries and their spouses, and major events that are considered National Special Security events.

The Secret Service work to counteract danger or threats and execute security operations that minimize, deter, and assertively act in response to vulnerabilities and threats that they identify. There are many special resources within the protective environment of the Secret Service that include the:

- o Emergency Response Team
- o Counter Surveillance Unit
- o Airspace Security Branch
- o Counter Sniper Team
- o Counter Assault Team
- o Medical Emergency Response Team
- o Hazardous Agent Mitigation
- o Magnetometer Operation Unit
- o Medical Emergency Response

Other resources that are specialized, and also provide protection from imminent threats, are explosive devices, as well as biological, chemical, nuclear and radiological materials, experts (Department of Homeland Security, 2019).

U.S. Secret Service Secrets

These are the agents who have to know everything about the President and Vice President, aside from their family members and friends. They are the closest to protect the president and vice president. They have an unusual intimacy with their charges. Their entire service is to watch every move of the president, vice president, their spouses and children, and even their pets. They are also responsible for watching every move of every person who interacts with the resident of the Oval Office, the VP, and family members. This includes heads of states who visit the White House, as well as all staff members, and anyone entering the White House living quarters for any reason, such as cleaning or picking up laundry, etc.

The History of the Secret Service

The United States Secret Service ranks as one of the most elite agencies in the world and is one of the oldest federal law enforcement agencies in the country. On July 5, 1865, the Secret Service Division was formed as part of the Department of the Treasury. The agency is now over 150 years old. The first Secret Service chief to be sworn into the agency was Chief William P. Wood.

Today, there are almost 7,000 employees of the Secret Service around the world. The field offices, aside from the United States, are Mexico, Canada, Europe, South America, Asia, and Africa (Secret Service, 2019).

The history of the Secret Service is quite interesting and ironically, it was Abraham Lincoln who, on the last day of his life April 14, 1865, signed legislation that authorized a government agency of the United States Secret Service.

However, the original authorization was not that the Secret Service guards the president. The reason Lincoln authorized the agency was for a mission that was far removed from presidential protection. The agency was to investigate and put a stop to counterfeit money. It was not until 1902 that the Secret Service took on the full-time responsibility to officially protect the president.

The mission first assigned to the agency was to stop counterfeit money, because by 1865, one-third to almost half of the money in circulation in America was counterfeit. Part of the reason was due to depending on an old system of state banks producing money using what the Federal Government provided in designs and paper. Although the country put forth a national currency in 1863, the federal money was very easy to replicate and counterfeit as that which state-produced.

After a major counterfeiter, Pete McCartney, produced what was rumored to be as much as $100,000 in counterfeit money, Lincoln called for a commission to come up with a solution to fix the counterfeit money problem. Hugh McCulloch, the then Treasury Secretary, put forth a solution to have a permanent and regular force that would enforce the law and have the counterfeiters put out of business (Blakemore, 2015).

The Secret Service first concentrated on the counterfeit money problem, and then expanded their mission in 1867 to include fraud committed by people against the government. Over time, the Secret Service took on more and more responsibility and acquired recognition as a distinctive organization given commissions and badges. In 1902 the Secret Service was given the full-time responsibility to protect the president after the assassination of President William McKinley in 1901. He was the third sitting president to have been assassinated, preceded by Abraham Lincoln (8865) and James Garfield (1881). This led to Congress requesting that the Secret Service protect the president.

Over the years, the responsibility of the Secret Service and their protection of the president evolved. During its history, the responsibilities grew to include the protection of the immediate family of the president, the protection of the vice president, the immediate family, and then adding the protection of major candidates for president, and Vice President and their families.

Not all the presidents and others who have had Secret Service assigned to them have been happy about the protection received by the Secret Service. President Theodore Roosevelt, General George Patton, and even President John F. Kennedy were not real fans of

U.S. Secret Service Secrets

the restrictiveness of the Secret Service and stated so in private as well as in public. However, the Secret Service continues to protect the president and is highly sensitive to the times when, even with all their efforts and unfortunate happenings, they thwart and foil repeated threats against the sitting Commander-in-Chief (Blakemore, 2015).

And yet the Secret Service still continues to bust counterfeiters. In 2016, the largest bust of counterfeit money that was found in Lima, Peru. Peru accounts for almost 60% of nearly $3 billion dollars of counterfeit money in the world. Along with counterfeit U.S. currency, $50,000 fake Euros were also discovered. The aftermath of the raid had 48 people arrested, six plants shut down, and eight manufacturing presses seized (Business Insider, 2016).

Applying to the Secret Service

Working as a Secret Service agent is extremely detailed and stressful. There are many who apply, but only a select few are chosen. Their training is intense, as it needs to be, in order to serve correctly and be prepared for anything that can happen while they are on duty. They are given stringent background checks, including employment history, police and military records, school transcripts, neighborhood references, and credit history. A candidate must be able to acquire a Top Secret clearance.

The hiring process and acceptance into the Secret Service is extensive and can take anywhere from six to nine months. The length of this process is for the applicant to have the ability to qualify for Top Secret clearance. Agents are placed in positions that are sensitive and relate to national security.

U.S. Secret Service Secrets

A candidate who is successful in joining the Secret Service has a 10-week training program to go through. This course gives the prospective agents the groundwork in criminal law and investigation methods. The Federal Law Enforcement Training Center in Glynco, GA is where the training program takes place. Upon completing the training course, it is followed by a 17-week Special Agent training program conducted in Washington D.C. at the Secret Service Training Academy. This training gives the candidate knowledge of procedures and policies as well as developing extensive knowledge of the Secret Service organization. Additional topics include emergency medicine, marksmanship, financial criminal activity, and device fraud. Both training programs must be passed by candidates on their first attempt (Criminal Justice Degree schools, 2019).

A potential Secret Service agent may be assigned anywhere and should be open to moving not only to anywhere in the United States, but anywhere in the world. They may be transferred to other venues in the nation or overseas as they gain experience.

They also must be willing to be away on business trips and from home for extended periods of time. Quite often this means weeks or even months. If a candidate is fluent in a foreign language, or more than one, they can be sent to an overseas post. Fluency in a foreign language may give a candidate a hiring advantage and may even earn a hiring bonus.

Other skills that can be beneficial are previous military or law enforcement experience. Agents must also have an understanding about how the government works, have a real concern about the well-being of government figures and their families, and at all times retain a professional attitude (Criminal Justice Degree schools, 2019).

Agents on the Job

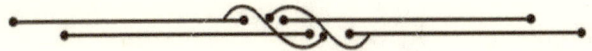

The job of a Secret Service agent is usually not a 9 to 5 one. An agent is typically assigned to work for a 24-hour shift and rotate shifts with other agents. Some agents are told on short notice that they have to travel. Some of these assignments can have an agent away from home for a month or more.

The agents are constantly learning through advanced training all through their careers. Their continued training covers instruction and refresher courses in requalifying for possession of firearms, as well as emergency medicine refresher courses. All training largely depends on the area that an agent is assigned to (Criminal Justice Degree schools, 2019).

Other types of crimes that the Secret Service investigates all threats made against persons the Secret Service protects, as well as financial crimes such as the theft or forgery of U.S. Treasury bonds, checks, or other securities; telecommunications fraud; credit card fraud; computer fraud and identity fraud, as well as other crimes that affect federally insured financial institutions (Secret Service, 2019).

The Secret Service employs other federal, state, and local agencies for assistance daily in protecting the president to maintain a safe environment. This is true when the President, Vice President, their families, or visiting dignitaries travel through cities and towns on their way to a conference or meeting.

Local and state law enforcement is crucial to the Secret Service, as they know the layout of the city or town that will be traveled through. When the president is set to travel to a certain location, the Secret Service sends an advance team of agents who work with the local and state law enforcement as well as officials of public safety of the host city. Working together, all the agencies jointly execute the necessary security measures necessary for the safety of the president and anyone traveling in the president's party (Secret Service, 2019).

The Secret Service consults on a regular basis with experts from outside agencies who utilize security techniques that are the most advanced and state-of-the-art. This is to enhance the ability of the agents to be as up-to-date as possible on all security methods that are available, as well as learning about the latest types of security breaches that are perpetrated by those who are less than scrupulous.

There are many areas of the government where the Secret Service is involved aside from the protection of the Executive Branch. As stated earlier in the chapter, the agency has a hand in many of the frauds that are perpetrated domestically as well as worldwide.

The agency itself has grown in the 150 plus years it has been in existence, and continues to do the work it was intended to do and more. The next chapters will

U.S. Secret Service Secrets

be about how the Secret Service protects the president, vice president, and their families, what is expected from the agency in the event of a national emergency, fun facts about the Secret Service, rumors and stories about the Secret Service over the years, and the new challenges they face in the evolving world of today.

Chapter 2: Direct Service to the President — Overall Service Provided to the President and Vice President Both on Domestic and International Travel

If you're a parent, have been a babysitter, or had an occasion to take care of an infant, toddler, or small child, you know what it's like to protect and watch over them. You make sure they're safe, and that no harm befalls them. You watch where they go and steer them clear of places they shouldn't be going and things that they shouldn't be putting into their mouths.

Watching a child over a long period can become exhaustive, and a guess here is, that's what naps are for, a time-out for the child and a rest reprieve for the caretaker.

U.S. Secret Service Secrets

Now, imagine the job of round-the-clock protection of grown adults who are free to move around, travel domestically and internationally, and at times make sudden, unscheduled stops or trips at a moment's notice. This is one of the many jobs that the Secret Service provide to the Executive Branch of our government, and one that is probably the most stressful of all the jobs any agent of the Secret Service can have. Even during the bedtime, whenever that is, of the president and others who are being protected, there is no time out. The protection is round the clock, even when the president is sleeping.

There are numerous ways that Secret Service agents protect the president, vice president, their immediate families and major candidates for president and vice president. The following will describe what Secret Service agents do for the president when he travels.

Agents inspect the travel location

U.S. Secret Service Secrets

The logistics and the planning that are involved in protecting the president when he travels, whether alone, with family members, or with the vice president are extensive and intense. The first line of the process, is the Secret Service agents assigned to the president and members of the White House staff visit the destination of the president as long as three months in advance and meet with local agencies, primarily local and state law enforcement agencies, and public officials.

In the time the agents and the White House staff visit the location, they have quite a bit to accomplish. The airport airspace must be clear during the arrival of the president on Air Force One, a motorcade route must be mapped through the town, the location of the nearest trauma hospital, and, in the event of an attack, a number of strategic safe locations for the president (Marum, Anna, 2015).

Problematic locals are forewarned they'll be watched

While the agents are perusing the travel location, they work with the local police in order to identify any threats that are possible and could be problematic during the course of the president's visit. These are known as "Class 3" threats, the most serious of possible threats. This category of threat is classified as Class 3 because those who fall under the category have threatened the president in the past. The Secret Service and local law enforcement feel there is a capability to carry out those threats. The agents contact those people, and they are put on notice and warned that they will be closely watched throughout the duration the president is in town.

The dogs do their job

As the arrival date of the president's trip draws closer, bomb-sniffing dogs are used to check each stop to be made on the route to be taken by the president. The nearby streets are cleared of all parked cars; notices are placed to warn there is no parking on the date or dates the president will be staying and traveling through pre-decided areas. The removal of parked cars prevents the ability to plant a bomb anywhere near the president's hotel. Canopies are set up at the areas where the president will exit his limousine to prevent exposure to crowds that would be located nearby (Marum, Anna, 2015).

Hospitals are put on notice

There needs to be a trauma center no more than 10 minutes away from where the president is staying and any location he will be in the area, i.e. a conference away from the hotel. Not only are hospitals put on notice, but an agent is stationed at each hospital. This is to make sure that an agent is ready to organize and coordinate with the physicians and other agents in the event there is a medical emergency.

U.S. Secret Service Secrets

The President's blood type travels in a bag

The Secret Service agents who travel with the president not only make sure there are hospitals at the ready in the event of a medical emergency, but the Presidential Protection Division (those agents who are responsible for protecting the lives of the president and his family) carries bags of the president's blood type in the event a transfusion is needed by the president (Bolluyt, 2018).

An extra plane is on standby

The president usually arrives at a destination in Air Force One. However, before the president's plane touches down, a plane used as a backup, similar to Air Force One, arrives at an undisclosed location in the event there is a mishap with the president's primary plane (Marum, Anna, 2015).

There are thousands of people who are involved

U.S. Secret Service Secrets

Not only are Air Force One and the standby plane used to fly in the president, but there at least six other planes that fly into the travel location. Some planes hold limousines and communication equipment, while helicopters and others will be flying in with hundreds of staff members and agents. Each time the president moves, there are thousands of people involved in the movement (Marum, Anna, 2015).

The President's limousine

As stated, some of the planes that fly into the travel location carry limousines for the motorcade. The most important limousine is the president's limousine. The limousine is heavily-armored, and is bulletproof as well as flat-tire-proof. The agents who drive the vehicle have intensive defense driving experience. The agents are trained to make 180-degree turns, enabling them to re-route a roadblock or avoid an explosion. When it's time for servicing, all the vehicles used go to the Secret Service maintenance garage. Other vehicles used by the agency are modified to make them more resistant to attack.

Highways are shut down

When the highways, freeways, or thruways are closed to allow the president's motorcade to travel through the city, the Secret Service drives the president the "wrong way" where the motorcade is a large, 20-vehicle entourage that travels in the empty lanes.

Hotels are chosen by the Secret Service

The hotels where the commander-in-chief stays are chosen by the Secret Service. They look for hotels where the environment can be controlled by them.

Background checks on all hotel staff

U.S. Secret Service Secrets

Prior to the president's arrival, agents perform background checks on all employees of the hotel. If anyone has a record of violence, even if it is a minor, fourth-degree assault charge that is a misdemeanor, they will be asked not to work the days the president is present.

Sneaking the president through the back door

The president is not usually led through the front of a hotel. Secret Service uses the back area of hotels, sometimes the loading dock area, and then lead the president through the maze of hallways, sometimes even the hotel kitchen, and up to his suite (Marum, Anna, 2015).

Hotel floors are cleared for the president, Secret Service, and staff

The floors above and below the floor the president's suite is located are isolated by the agents. Only the president's detail will be allowed to stay in these rooms or enter and leave these floors (Marum, Anna, 2015).

All electronics and telephones are removed

Prior to the arrival of the president to the hotel suite, a thorough and complete sweep of all the rooms the president will be is performed by the agents. There is a check for concealed explosives and bugging devices. All pictures that are hanging on the walls in the rooms are taken apart to make sure that nothing has been hidden in the frames. Bulletproof plastic is used to cover all the windows, and all phones and television are removed. This is done to ensure that the room is emptied of all electronics that can possibly be used to wiretap and eavesdrop. The agents replace all the electronics with their own electronics that are secure.

The president is protected at three perimeters

U.S. Secret Service Secrets

The Secret Service agents form three security perimeters to surround the president. The outer perimeter is formed by the local law enforcement, the middle perimeter is made up by general Secret Service agents, and the perimeter closest to the president is made up by the Presidential Protective Division agents who will provide the shield that is the innermost to the president (Marum, Anna, 2015).

They watch the food

The president usually travels with his own food. There are also cooks and servers who travel with the president. They purchase the groceries and prepare all the food the president will eat. The preparation is done separately in a kitchen that is available and Secret Service agents observe the preparation to make sure there is no interference from outsiders (Marum, Anna, 2015).

The Secret Service is always there

U.S. Secret Service Secrets

The Secret Service agents never leave the president alone, even in the restroom, bathroom, doctor's office, or any place one would normally have some privacy. The president is never alone and does not enter any room alone. Even during a medical procedure, an agent is always present in the room, armed with a gun
(Bolluyt, 2018).

These procedures and steps taken and followed to the letter by the Secret Service with regards to protecting the president, when traveling to events, rallies, conferences, addressing the United Nations in New York City, or any other function that takes him out of the White House.

Although the president is protected even within the White House and all government buildings he enters, special care is taken when the president is on the road domestically, or to international meetings like the G-

U.S. Secret Service Secrets

20 Summit in Germany, G-2 Summit in Italy, Saudi Arabia, or Viet Nam, making the job of protecting the president by the Secret Service agents the most stressful position an agent can have.

Chapter 3: What Does the Secret Service Do in the Event of a National Emergency

Over the course of the history of the Secret Service, there have been emergencies that have influenced the safety of the president, vice president, and their families, as well as the well-being of the American people.

The Secret Service are trained to react at a moment's notice. Whether it is a threat, indirect or direct, to the President, or the hijacking of airplanes and using them as weapons of attack against our country, the Secret Service must react and react quickly. For those who are in the agency, there is no room for error when an emergency is a matter of life or death to anyone in their charge and those who are affected by their actions.

U.S. Secret Service Secrets

September 11, 2001 was a travel day for President George W. Bush. He was on his way to Florida to visit with schoolchildren. While en route, he is informed that a passenger jet had crashed into one of the towers of the World Trade Center in lower Manhattan, New York City. Although this had happened, he continued to proceed with the visit to meet the schoolchildren. At this point, the crashing of an airplane into the World Trade Center was an unfortunate accident that would be dealt with by local law enforcement of the NYPD, the fire department FDNY, and first responders. Bush would be kept informed (History.com Editors, 2019).

The purpose of President Bush's trip was to promote an education bill. The visit to the Booker Elementary School in Sarasota, FL had been pre-arranged. As was usual, the President had been given a security briefing scheduled earlier that morning. That day there had been an increased but non-specific threat of a terrorist attack. The President was warned, but even with this information he continued on to the school. Transiting from his hotel to the school is when his aides let the president know that the jet had crashed into the North Tower of the World Trade Center at 8:46 am. At this point, Bush was in his limousine as part of the usual motorcade that accompanies the President during any trip outside of the White House driving towards the school.

When Bush arrived at the school with his Secret Service detail, the classroom was empty. The news footage of the North Tower and the plane crash was being reported on the television screens in the school. Bush was ushered into the classroom by Secret Service to meet with the schoolchildren who had arrived and were taking their seats. The children were first graders. The second plane had not yet hit the Towers (History.com Editors, 2019).

The visit to the school was being videotaped. At 9:06 am Andrew Card, the White House Chief of Staff entered the classroom. He quietly whispered to the President that a second airplane had struck the World Trade Center. He stated quietly that the nation was under attack and it was not yet known who the entity was or the why of the attack (History.com Editors, 2019).

There were a few minutes of maintaining calm so as not to alarm the children. Once the President fulfilled his meeting, his Secret Service detail took charge. He was brought to an empty classroom and watched to news reports of the attacks. Bush, Vice President, Dick Cheney, and the Governor of New York, George Pataki, consulted via telephone. After making the first of many live announcements over that day, Secret Service agents rushed Bush to Air Force One, which was waiting at Sarasota's airport. He was on his way to the airport when reports of a third attack, this one on the Pentagon in Washington, D.C., had occurred.

Safely aboard Air Force One, the pilot flew in circles while the Bush and Cheney discussed where the safest place for Air Force One to land and be at this time. The Secret Service had the plane stop over at an air base in Louisiana, then proceeded to Offutt Air Force Base in Nebraska. By the early evening just before 7 pm, President Bush had returned to Washington (History.com Editors, 2019).

This narrative of the events of 9/11 2001 seemed to have the American public believe that the worst of the situation was in New York City at the World Trade Center Towers, where United Flight 175 and American Airlines Flight 11 crashed into the Twin Towers, at the Pentagon where American Airlines Flight 77 had crashed, and a field in Shanksville, PA where a fourth plane, Flight 93 had crashed (Arkin, William M & Windrem, Robert, 2016).

What Americans and the rest of the world did not know was that there was a more complicated situation that involved live nuclear weapons and inadequate communications equipment, and that the President himself was in a more dangerous position than was publicly realized.

What no one was aware of was when Air Force One took off from Sarasota to get Bush to a safe place, the annual "Global Guardian" war game was in full swing. Loaded onboard intercontinental bombers in North Dakota, Missouri, and Louisiana were three dozen real nuclear weapons. The war games necessitated that Air Force One flew as high as 48,000 feet. Bush was essentially in orbit. The plane was also low on fuel with no real destination. It was not until Admiral Richard Mies, the commander of STRATCOM, the U.S. Strategic Command stopped the exercises when he became aware of the attacks in New York and Washington. This allowed for Air Force One to head to Barksdale, LA, one of the primary B-52 bomber bases in the world (Arkin, William M & Windrem, Robert, 2016).

At the time all this was happening, the Secret Service agents who were on board were getting directions from various high-ranking military personnel, senior members of the White House staff, and from Bush. Their sole purpose was to continue to protect President Bush and help in the decisions that were made to get the President to a safe place and get Air Force One refueled.

The Secret Service and the president's security team dissuaded Bush from returning to Washington and the White House. They were still unclear as to whether there were other planes ready to attack. They knew that if the Pentagon had already been struck, the White House could be next (Arkin, William M & Windrem, Robert, 2016).

There was the problem of the nuclear weapons on one hand, and the fear that there was a possibility there were more attackers who could target the air base where the nuclear weapons were. Air Force One wanted to land at Barksdale and there was a mad dash by munitions specialists to complete the task of unloading the bombers. The other problem was there was no communication between Air Force One and anyone else. Secret Service and the Air Force One pilot wanted all cell phones to be turned off so the plane could not be tracked. Bush was able to speak with Dick Cheney who was at the Mount Weather facility, but he couldn't speak to his wife for almost three hours. She was located at the Capitol Building.

Vladimir Putin wanted to speak with Bush. It was by coincidence that a nuclear war exercise was also being conducted by the Russians. Russian intelligence had distinguished there to be telltale signs of heightened American force position. Putin wanted to know a DEFCON 3 was being prepared by the United States, but the White House and Air Force One could not communicate (Arkin, William M & Windrem, Robert, 2016).

While the Secret Service and the military were trying to get Bush to a secure location, Rod Paige, the Education Secretary who had traveled with Bush on Air Force One to meet with other officials to talk about the education bill, was left behind on the tarmac at Sarasota, FL. He rented a car and drove back to Washington D.C.

A government plane carrying Attorney General John Ashcroft tried to land in Washington D.C., but the FAA turned his plane away.

The attack on 9/11 exposed weaknesses that had not been noted in the past and now were being dealt with. Government protocol the preparations for security in case of another attack on the capital was put into place (Arkin, William M & Windrem, Robert, 2016).

Each time an emergency has arisen, like the assassination attempt on Ronald Reagan in 1981, a

U.S. Secret Service Secrets

1983 war game when the Russians were mistaken and thought it was the real thing, and finally the confusion of 9/11, the Secret Service and other law enforcement agencies of the government rethink and upgrade the security measures needed to protect the president, as well as other individuals, keep communication lines open both domestically and internationally, and continue to strive for the best possible security measures allowing for the Secret Service to perform their job in the very best way possible.

Chapter 4: Fun Facts about the U.S. Secret Service

A most secretive group, one wonders *who is the Secret Service?* Forever watching, they stay close to their charges. The Secret Service is the main protection agency of the president, vice president, their families, foreign dignitaries, and presidential hopefuls.

However, looking at the behind the scenes of American politics, the Secret Service is there almost all the time. This chapter is full of interesting facts that may surprise the reader. Some of the facts are newer information, and others are historical. Because the origins of the Secret Service is part of the Department of the Treasury and continues to be to this day, there are many interesting stories about the agency and how it has been involved with the presidency and politics.

U.S. Secret Service Secrets

Secret Service established by President Abraham Lincoln

As you've read previously, President Abraham Lincoln authorized the Secret Service on April 14, 1865, the day of President Lincoln's assassination. The purpose of the Secret Service was because of the abundance of counterfeit money being distributed throughout the United States. It was unfortunate that the Secret Service was only just authorized and there had been no real protection for President Lincoln except for one police officer. History may have been different if it were not for the assassination.

The Secret Service's duties were broadened to handle the perpetration of mass frauds by any person against the United States government, such as the Ku Klux Klan among others.

The agency would take the responsibility of protecting the president in 1894, although this was done informally until 1902 when it became permanent. (Ranker News, 2019).

The FBI is an offshoot of the Secret Service

The Department of Justice (DOJ) wanted to conduct investigations nationally and needed agents to carry out these investigations. They pulled nine Secret Service agents to manage the investigations. The Bureau of Investigation was the name given to the organization started with the nine agents, and would ultimately become the Federal Bureau of Investigation, known as the FBI (Ranker News, 2019).

There have never been traitorous activities in the Secret Service

Unlike the FBI, the National Security Agency (NSA), and the Central Intelligence Agency (CIA) that have had turncoats, traitors, and infiltration by devious foreign agents, there has never been a Secret Service agent who misused their rank and association with the agency.

Franklin Delano Roosevelt – the 32nd President of the United States

The public image of President Franklin Delano Roosevelt, known as FDR, was protected by the Secret Service by hiding his infirmity. At the age of 21, Roosevelt contracted polio and was not able to walk without assistance, and was to sit in a wheelchair most of the time. If there were photos that were undesirable, like agents carrying Roosevelt because his wheelchair couldn't roll over certain types of ground, Secret Service agents would often chase the photographer. Their cameras were either seized or damaged "accidentally" (Ranker News, 2019).

Al Capone's car was useful to the Secret Service

FDR was having his auto, the Sunshine Special, upgraded per the direction of the Secret Service in order to ensure his protection. The upgrades were being done after Pearl Harbor and there were limited funds to perform the necessary work. While they were waiting for the upgrades to be completed, the Secret Service was able to use a vehicle that had formerly been used by Al Capone, an infamous gangster. It fit the bill perfectly.

The additional "Air Force One"

As read previously, when the president travels, the Secret Service uses Air Force One to transport him, and an additional plane is flown to an undisclosed location as a backup in case of an accident that would necessitate using the second plane. The location of the second plane is only known to the Secret Service (Ranker News, 2019).

U.S. Secret Service Secrets

President and VP families were not protected until 1917

The Secret Service agency added the families of presidents and vice presidents in 1917. Then, the White House police, created by President Warren G. Harding, was assigned to protect the living quarters of the president and vice president. The responsibility of protecting the premises would eventually become another responsibility of the Secret Service.

Three service phases

Secret Service agents have to work at the office for three years before they are involved in fieldwork. This prepares them for the challenges that are involved in fieldwork, which lasts 4-7 years. In the final phase, an agent returns to office work or is promoted to a higher position (Brightside, 2014-2019).

U.S. Secret Service Secrets

Their training involves life or death and always being ready to provide first aid

The Secret Service agents, prior to an important event, envision and rehearse all possible and probable situations of shootouts and murder attempts. Bullets are made specifically for training sessions such as these. Additionally, all agents go through a course for skills development every eight weeks.

Every agent has basic medical skills, and are ready to save someone's life even before an ambulance arrives or before they get to a hospital. Each route the president takes must have a hospital always no more than 10 minutes away.

The Sunglasses

Many have always wondered about the sunglasses. Are they worn so that potential shooters or those persons the agents want to keep their eye on have no idea where the agents are looking? No, not really. Actually, they are used for the most practical reason—to shield their eyes from the sun (Ranker News, 2019).

However, there are those agents who do not use sunglasses during their missions. The feeling is, something important can be missed due to either lack of light or glare. (Brightside, 2014-2019).

Washington D.C. is only one place where the Secret Service has offices

The Secret Service has many field offices in all 50 states and some U.S. territories, including Puerto Rico and Guam. In California alone, there are nine offices in the state. There are also a number of international branches in several foreign countries, including Russia.

U.S. Secret Service Secrets

The agency keeps its headquarters a secret. Their headquarters are located in Washington D.C. The building has no identifying signs; no trash cans nearby and is located on a street with a short name: H Street (Ranker News, 2019) (Brightside, 2014-2019).

Acting as a Secret Service agent

Diane Lane, Clint Eastwood, Michael Douglas, Kevin Costner, Eva Longoria, Gerald Butler, Rene Russo, and many others have played a Secret Service agent in numerous films. One actor who played a Secret Service agent four times in different films ended up being protected by them in real life. That actor became the 40th President of the United States: Ronald Reagan.

There was only one Secret Service agent fatality while protecting a President: the attempted assassination of President Harry S. Truman

U.S. Secret Service Secrets

President Harry S. Truman and his family were residing at Blair House, the guest house used for visitors not far from the White House. Truman wanted to have a balcony added to the second-floor south portico, now known as the Truman Balcony. Although the addition was not a popular one, it allowed the First Family to be able to have more living space. Thus, the family moved over to Blair House until the renovations were completed.

Two Puerto Rican nationalists, Griselio Torresola and Oscar Collazo, tried an attempt on Truman's life at Blair House on November 1, 1950. Outside on the street, Torresola killed Leslie Coffelt, a White House policeman. Coffelt shot and killed Torresola before he died. Collazo was stopped from entering the house and was wounded. Collazo was tried and found guilty of attempted murder. Originally sentenced to death, Truman commuted his sentence to life in prison (Ranker News, 2019).

U.S. Secret Service Secrets

A referendum held in Puerto Rico on a new constitution was allowed by President Truman to determine the relationship status to the U.S. A majority of 82 percent of the people voted for a new constitution for the Estado Libre Asociado, a continuation of an associated free state.

Secret Service wards have code names

The Secret Service assigns code names to the president and his family members, all starting with the same letter. President Barack Obama and his family were given the letter "R" to choose code names. Obama chose "Renegade," Michelle Obama chose the code name "Renaissance," and their daughters were "Radiance" and "Rosebud" (Ranker News, 2019).

Jimmy Carter was "Deacon," George H.W. Bush was "Gray Wolf," Bill Clinton was "Eagle," George W. Bush was "Acrobat," John F. Kennedy was "Lancer," and Richard Nixon was "Searchlight" (Brightside, 2014-2019).

The man with a knife in the same elevator as Barack Obama – myth or truth?

Unfortunately, it's the truth. President Obama was with an armed officer riding in an elevator when a man with a knife entered the grounds of the White House by jumping the fence (Brightside, 2014-2019).

Watch the Secret Service hands

The next time you see a photo of a Secret Service agent within the protection distance from the president or vice president, watch their hands. They are always at the ready. Each of them may have a different finger position, but the meaning is the same. Their hands are unencumbered and at the ready to react rapidly and raise their weapon (Brightside, 2014-2019).

Filming of presidential motorcades

Filming of the president's motorcade is done in the event that something goes wrong. This is a result of the assassination of President John F. Kennedy in 1963. The Zapruder film that memorialized the event was controversial, but was invaluable in assisting the Secret Service to see and understand how rapidly an event can get out of control.

Agents study footage of that event today as a part of their training. Current presidential motorcades are filmed in the event there is an attack and the film is needed to review it (Bolluyt, 2018).

President and vice president cannot opt out of Secret Service security

The president and vice president do not have a choice in being guarded by the Secret Service. They are guarded 24/7/365, no exception. They cannot refuse Secret Service supervision. They can, however, hire private security after their term in office ends (Bolluyt, 2018).

The electronic crimes task force

The Secret Service investigates any computer fraud or hacking crimes in additional their continuing efforts to prevent counterfeiting. The agency plays a crucial role in the nation's critical infrastructures, especially in the areas of finance, cyber, and banking. They also oversee transnational organized crime. These corrupt organizations target financial institutions and individuals of the U.S.

Today, investigative experts, intelligence analysts, and forensics experts give a quick response and crucial information in support of criminal investigations, infrastructure protection, and financial analysis (Secret Service , 2019).

State-of-the-art forensics unit

The Secret service houses the world's largest ink library as well as audio enhancement and high-tech video equipment. The agency also assisted in cases involving exploited and missing children, authorized by President Bill Clinton in 1994.

The next chapter will continue to reveal more of the many stories and facts that are part of the Secret Service's history.

Chapter 5: Rumors and Stories of the Secret Service over the Years

In the last chapter, there were fun facts about the Secret Service, some that are public knowledge and some that may have been a surprise.

There are rumors and stories about the Secret Service because their secrecy can sometimes spark them. Here are some rumors and stories about the agency.

Mount Weather – myth or truth?

Mount Weather is used to hide one government representative in an underground bunker in the mountain during an event where other state officials meet. If terrorists think they will be able to kill the top level of the government, it probably won't happen. This is the facility where Dick Cheney was taken on September 11, 2001, during the attack on the World Trade Center.

U.S. Secret Service Secrets

The Mount Weather Emergency Operations Center located in the Commonwealth of Virginia is used for the Federal Emergency Management Agency (FEMA) as a center of operations. The High Point Special Facility (HPSF) is another name for the center, and since 1991 the name preferred is SF.

In the event of a national disaster, it is a key relocation site for civilian and military officials of the highest level. It plays a chief role in the continuity of government. The FEMA National Radio System (FNARS) is a radio system that is high frequency and connects to most states' United States military and public federal safety agencies. The president has access to the Emergency Alert System via FNARS.

On December 1, 1974, TWA Flight 514 crashed into Mount Weather facility. The Washington Post brought the site into the public eye when this event happened.

Does the Oval Office have motion sensors in the floor?

There are many rules that Secret Service agents, especially the President's, detail. One of the most important of those rules is that the president should not be left alone. If the president requests that he would like to stay alone in the Oval Office minus the agents, the Secret Service can trace any movement and possible threat by monitoring the sensors in the floor.

Agents swear to die for their president – myth

This is a myth. No such oath exists in the annals of the Secret Service. Only in Hollywood. Agents are trained to take a bullet for the president, but there is no oath to do so. The possibility that something could happen is understood. Everyone works to the common goal of avoiding a deadly situation.

When did the Secret Service become responsible for presidential candidates?

The assassination of Robert F. Kennedy in 1968 was the reason that Congress authorized protection of major candidates running for the presidency and vice presidency. Within 120 days of the general election, there is protection for candidates and nominees. The Secretary of Homeland Security, in conjunction with an advisory committee, identifies those candidates who receive Secret Service protection. This is according to 18 United States Code § 3056 (Brown, Heather, 2015).

The badges of the Secret Service

The Secret Service badge is worn with tremendous pride by its owner and affirms fulfilling the duties and responsibilities of the Secret Service personnel, and the duty they are trusted to perform.

U.S. Secret Service Secrets

The Secret Service badges were first introduced in 1869 to be worn by operatives of the agency. The badges were instituted during the term of Hiram C. Whitley, who was Chief of the Secret Service in 1869. He gave permission that operatives get their own badges if they wanted to wear them. The first standard badge was issued by the Secret Service in 1873. The badges were designed and manufactured by a private firm. Unfortunately, there are no records of the actual appearance of the first badges.

Service Star of 1875 and 1890

Chief Whitley requested that the Bureau of Engraving and Printing design a new badge in 1875. The official emblem, the "Service Star," is the first to feature the star's five points, each of which represents the agency's five core values: duty, justice, honesty, courage, and loyalty (Secret Service, 2019).

The badge was redesigned in 1890 for the Secret Service. The badge was designed smaller, making it easier to carry in the commission books of the agents.

The Badges of the Uniformed Division – White House Police

These badges were different in appearance than the five-point Secret Service badges. Gold in tone and designed as a shield, the first badge was for the Uniformed Division, issued in 1922. Between 1940 and 1978, there have been seven redesigned badges (Secret Service, 2019).

Badge consistency – 1971

The re-design of the Secret Service badge in 1971 was so that all law enforcement agencies' badges within the Department of the Treasury were consistent in design. The new badge was created by the Secret Service's graphic artists. The badge was a shield in design with the five-point star remaining and embedded within the new design.

Special Agent Badge – 2003

A Special Agent badge was designed and introduced in 2003 (Secret Service, 2019).

Guarding the Presidents

Presidents and agents share similar interests

President Ronald Reagan was an avid horse lover and rode on his ranch in California whenever possible. This was an activity that Reagan shared with his Secret Service agent John Barletta. They spent hours together talking and riding. For Barletta, this still involved his job to watch over his charge, and the wide open spaces they rode through made it difficult. It was all private land of Reagan's ranch, which made protecting Reagan a bit easier (Satore, 2019).

Presidential hobbies can be a pain

A regular jogger by the time he came to the White House in 1992, Bill Clinton made it somewhat difficult for the Secret Service to direct his jogging activities. While the beginning of his presidency proved he wasn't that fast, and the agents at first did not have to be in the best of shape, it soon became evident that the agents in Clinton's detail would have to step it up.

The experience of taking a sitting president running out in public, when there can be anyone out there with ill intentions who can harm the president, is a nightmare for any Secret Service agent. The agents had to carry their radios and guns, scanning the streets while running.

The Secret Service tried to keep Clinton safe on his jogs and suggested the president run at a military base on a track. Clinton refused. He felt that jogging was for health and for public relations, and he wanted to be seen by the public. Secret Service agents were placed at various streets throughout Washington D.C. and in other cities when Clinton traveled. The agents also mapped out routes that were approved and arranged, for "guest runs" with well-connected citizens. (Satore, 2019)

Awkward situations for agents

President Lyndon Johnson was considered ill-mannered, to put it mildly, and was angered when agents didn't do as he asked. There was an incident when Johnson, while being driven to an event, ordered an agent to jump the curb because they were running late. The agent did not want to and refused. They were fired the next day. There was an intervention by Johnson's secretary and that saved their job.

U.S. Secret Service Secrets

Another instance of Johnson treating Secret Service agents like hired hands was described by a former Secret Service agent. When Johnson let his dog Yukie out, he shouted "Secret Service! You can throw Yukie back in when he's finished." This type of behavior was resented and there was never a *please* or *thank you* offered. The night of this particular request, it had been raining and Yukie became very muddy while doing his business. The agent brought Yukie back to the house. The next morning, Johnson woke up to a muddy mess on his silk bed sheets. The agents were told that in the future when they brought the dog back inside after being out, to clean him up first (Satore, 2019).

An agent protecting a vice president took another approach to the dog walking demands. When Vice President Hubert Humphrey asked him to walk his dog, the agent told Humphrey that he and other Secret Service agents were not allowed to walk a dog,

but told Humphrey he would be happy to walk him instead
(Satore, 2019).

Agents as babysitters

When Jimmy Carter was elected, his daughter Amy was only 9 years old. For the Secret Service detail guarding Amy, supervising her evening activities, accompanying her to friends' homes, and putting in extra hours to do so were all part of the job. There were times when Amy wanted to visit with friends after school rather than go directly home, changing the orders of the agents who were instructed to bring her directly home. Amy would call her father and put him on the phone. The agents were then instructed to take her wherever she wanted to go.

Amy would sometimes have agents clean up her mess after she knowingly would throw crumbs on the floor. However, her misdeeds were mild in comparison to her brother James Carter III's. Chip, as he was known, who had recently separated from his wife, went out drinking and picking up women, then bringing them back to the White House. Totally unruly, he was the least liked of the presidential children the Secret Service ever protected.

The Secret Service has a history rich with facts and anecdotes. Some of them are known and others not known. And there are probably some that we, as the public, will never know. The operative word for Secret Service is *secret*.

Chapter 6: The Secret Service Today

No one is perfect. Not even the Secret Service. Three years ago, the U.S. Secret Service grappled with a number of controversies that were damaging and included a breakdown in security, a serious breach of protocol for an agency whose sole purpose is the security of the highest regard. An investigation by Congress and a report that was bipartisan about the agency, showed that it was in a stage of crisis, was what Congress determined. One of the primary causes of the difficulties the agency was having was discovered by lawmakers and identified as budget cuts.

The Secret Service has worked to turn the tide on the situation since the report was released, and now the agency has been faced with another challenge: the presidency of Donald Trump.

U.S. Secret Service Secrets

The president's team and the Secret Service have faced some problems. One of them was an attorney for Trump who tried to lay blame on the agency for the Trump Tower meeting, which is now infamous for having an association with a Russian lawyer. Making a rare statement and entry into a political debate, the Secret Service was prompted to do so in defense of the agents' actions (Benen, 2017).

Another issue that has made it a difficult task to keep Trump safe is the multilayered security system around the Mar-a-Lago property when the president is in town. This commentary is based on Secret Service practices during four visits in February and March of 2017. A new study reported by a nonpartisan congressional watchdog group spotlights the challenges the Secret Service have in the ability to protect Trump (Siegel, Benjamin and Bruggerman, Lucien, 2019).

U.S. Secret Service Secrets

The Government Accountability Office (GAP) conducted the study after it was reported that there were discussions of national security with Japanese Prime Minister Shinzo Abe as well as club dinner guests. The discussion was in reference to how secure the president was at Mar-a-Lago after a North Korean missile test. It was discovered that the Secret Service gives a number of layers of security to Trump when he is in town and residing at the club.

Information about the security system around the club performed by the Secret Service, Coast Guard, and local law enforcement patrolling the entrances and adjoining waterways, and other security information, was detailed in the report.

The discussion at a dinner with Trump and Prime Minister Abe gave private citizens who had no security clearances a chance to overhear classified or sensitive national security information. Needless to say, the discussion as to how security is performed by the Secret Service to the president when he is in residence at Mar-a-Lago, did not make the agency very happy. The entire purpose of them keeping their operation and protection methods secret is to deter anyone who wanted to harm the president or perpetrate an attack. Revealing how the president is guarded with intimate details is not what the Secret Service had planned (Benen, 2017).

However, keeping their charges maintained is not the only challenge that has faced the Secret Service. During the week of March 11-18, 2017, the laptop of a special agent was stolen. In it were government documents that were sensitive in content, such as the floor plans to Trump Tower and details of Hillary Clinton's private email server investigation (Rogan, Tom, 2017).

Yet another incident to blemish the record of the Secret Service was an intruder on the White House grounds on March 10, 2017. The intruder was on the grounds for 15 minutes before he was finally caught.

Both of these incidents have had the Secret Service demand that the agents' laptops be stored in a location that is safe and not easy to access. The agency also takes responsibility that intruders be detained quickly (Rogan, Tom, 2017).

Neither case was connected and there was no corresponding plot. What might have happened had they been is not too hard to imagine. If either event had involved a terrorist group skilled in theft, using the information contained in the Secret Service posts in the Trump Tower, it might have been able to assassinate the president. Another scenario is that the lone intruder was joined by four or five other intruders, all terrorists. This would have put Trump at risk (Rogan, Tom, 2017).

U.S. Secret Service Secrets

The laptop theft was inexcusable but guarding the president at the White House is not so easy. The White House was designed to be accessible, the people's house, not for security. The accessibility is why the White House is located in the middle of a major city. This causes demanding security challenges to the Secret Service in protecting the president while he is in the Oval Office.

Tens of thousands of individuals pass by the White House unscreened each day. There are 121 meters between Pennsylvania Avenue to the unscreened citizens. Because of the difficulty in protecting the president, the Secret Service would use Mount Weather, the underground bunker, to house the president if it were up to them (Siegel, Benjamin and Bruggerman, Lucien, 2019).

The Secret Service has set out to improve what happened two years ago. Today, they have maintained their mission even during the recent government shutdown. Another attempt by an intruder, Christopher Henry-Alexander Davis of Herndon, VA, to access the White House on February 18, 2019, was thwarted by a Secret Service agent who struggled with the intruder, claiming he had an appointment with President Trump.

The intruder was subdued, arrested, and charged with resisting arrest and assault of a Secret Service Agent.

The challenges that face the Secret Service are constant. Every moment of each day they protect the president, vice president and their families, visiting dignitaries and the like is a continuous job that is stressful, detailed, at times complicated, and expected to be performed without a glitch.

Their painstaking work in protection, as well as their continued work uprooting counterfeiters, and fighting cybercrimes will continue. President Lincoln would be proud.

U.S. Secret Service Secrets

Conclusion

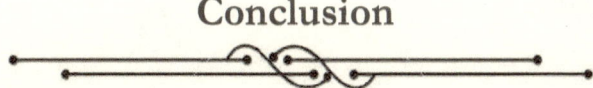

Thank for reading *U.S. Secret Service Secrets: Interesting Facts About American Agents and Their Service to the Nation.* This e-book was written with the hope of being as informative as possible about the Secret Service agents, men, and women who serve the agency as well as other government branches of our country every day.

The Secret Service, primarily formed to stop the counterfeiting of money in the United States post-Civil War, has evolved to incorporate the agency in many facets of the government and protect against the frauds and dangers that are a part of our world today. One of the most important duties of the Secret Service is the protection of the President, Vice President, and their families. Additionally, they are also responsible to protect any visiting dignitaries and their spouses.

Performing the duties of the Secret Service as protector is probably one of the most stressful jobs one can take on. Their every thought process and move must involve the safety of another human being. Needless to say, the job of agents assigned to the Presidential Protective Division, the president's personal detail, can be extremely intense and stressful.

However, there are other positions within the Secret Service. The agency is still involved with unscrupulous money counterfeiters, as well as having Counter Surveillance Unit, Airspace Security Branch, Counter Sniper Team, Counter Assault Team, and many other areas that the Secret Service is involved in and serves.

Finally, if you found this book enjoyable, a review on Amazon is always appreciated!

Michelle L. Fischer

Connect with us on our Facebook page
www.facebook.com/bluesourceandfriends and stay
tuned to our latest book promotions and free
giveaways.